AFRICA:
POSTCOLONIAL
CONFLICT

DAVID DOWNING

Deleted

Chicago, Illinois

For information, address the publisher
Raintree
100 N. LaSalle, Suite 1200, Chicago, IL 60602

Library of Congress Cataloging-in-Publication Data:
Downing, David, 1946-
  Africa : postcolonial conflict / David Downing.
      p. cm. -- (Troubled world)
Summary: Describes political, economic, religious, and other problems
which plague the entire continent of Africa today, and their sources in
European colonial rule in the nineteenth and twentieth centuries.
Includes bibliographical references (p.) and index.
  ISBN 1-4109-0183-1
  1. Africa--Politics and government--1960---Juvenile literature. 2.
Africa--Social conditions--1960---Juvenile literature. [1.
Africa--Politics and government--1960- 2. Africa--Social
conditions--1960-] I. Title. II. Series.
  DT30.5.D69 2003
  960.3'2--dc21
                              2003002154

Printed and bound in China by South China Printing Company.

08 07 06 05 04
10 9 8 7 6 5 4 3 2 1

Acknowledgments
The publishers would like to thank the following for permission to reproduce photographs:
pp. 6, 16, 24, 26, 27, 28, 32, 54 Popperfoto; pp. 9, 15, 18, 19, 31, 37, 50, 53, 55, 57 Corbis: 57
(Adrian Arbib), 37 (Baci), 50 (Howard Davies), 9 (Owen Franken), 53 (Bill Gentile), 15 (Daniel
Laine), 18 (Neal Preston),19 (Chris Rainier), 31 (David Turnley); pp. 10, 14, 21, 35, 39, 40, 42,
43, 45, 46, 48, 49 Popperfoto (Reuters); p. 23 Topham/AP; p. 30 Popperfoto (UPI); p.38
Popperfoto (Alexander Joe); p. 59 Still pictures (Ron Giling).

Cover photograph of Zairean refugees heading toward the Rwandan border, November
1996. Reproduced with permission of Topham/AP.

Every effort has been made to contact copyright holders of any material reproduced in this
book. Any omissions will be rectified in subsequent printings if notice is given to the publishers.

Contents

Words that appear in the text in bold, **like this**, are explained in the glossary.

Troubled Continent

Africa is the world's second largest continent, slightly more than three times the size of the United States. Much of Africa lies within the tropics, but there is considerable geographical diversity: the dense rain forests of the Congo, the fertile hills of the Great Rift Valley, the dry grasslands of the savanna, and the arid deserts of the Sahara and Kalahari.

At the beginning of 2003, there were 900 million Africans. In the last 40 years, the population of Africa has increased by 300 percent, compared with a population increase of 60 percent in the United States over the same period. By 2025 the continent is predicted to be home to a fifth of the world's people. Africa's people are as varied as its geography. Over 1,000 languages are spoken by an even larger number of social groupings—variously called **tribes, clans,** or **ethnic** groups. Over the last half century, these groupings have been divided up, often unevenly, into 53 states or countries.

The states that lie to the north of the Sahara Desert, mostly **Muslim** and populated by Arabic-speaking peoples, have much closer ties to the Middle East than the rest of Africa. This book is concerned with the troubled history of the states that lie between the Sahara Desert and South Africa, those states that form the bulk of black Africa. (South Africa's highly distinctive recent history has earned it a book of its own in this series.)

History

Until about 1,000 years ago, this area of Africa was a land of many different tribes with a few larger kingdoms. It had little contact with the rest of the world. Over the next 900 years, it was slowly penetrated by other, more outgoing cultures, principally the **Arabs** of the Middle East and the seafaring nations of northwest Europe. These intruders brought their religions—**Islam** in the north and east, **Christianity** in much of the rest—and the slave trade. A few settled in the land, but most were content to take the continent's riches home with them. At the end of the 1800s, most of Africa was formally divided into European **colonies**, under the direct rule of the European **colonial** powers.

This colonial period ended, with a few exceptions, in the late 1950s and early 1960s. The European administrators went home, and most of the newly independent countries set out to develop their economies along **free enterprise** lines and establish systems of government. There have been some successes. A few economies have flourished, at least for a while, and there are signs that **democracy** has taken root in some countries. But mostly there have been failures. Over the last 40 years, many African countries have succumbed to brutal dictators, and economic progress has been either minimal or nonexistent. As poverty and hopelessness have spread, violence has erupted both within and between states. Many millions of ordinary Africans have had their already difficult lives made worse by fear and tragedy.

Why has this happened? How has Africa south of the Sahara become a place in crisis? We must begin with the first real turning point of modern African history, independence from colonial rule.

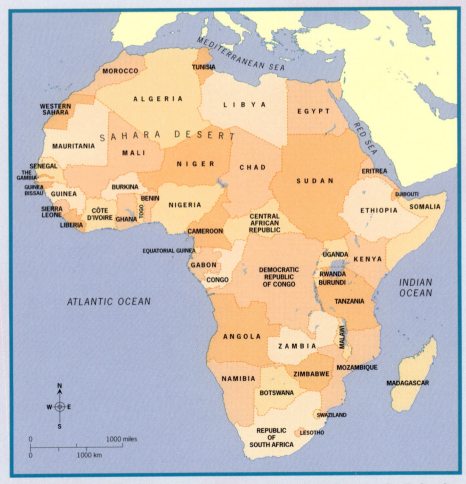

Africa today. All of the countries are now free from colonial rule.

Turning Point: Independence

Europeans first came to **sub-Saharan Africa** in the 1400s. For the next 400 years, they confined themselves to building settlements on the coasts and stealing or trading everything from gold to human beings. It was not until the late 19th century, with the slave trade abolished and most of the continent explored, mapped, and divided, that the European powers began to govern Africa on a daily basis. The period of **colonial** rule lasted, in most cases, considerably less than a century. Zambia, for example, was first subjected to white colonial rule in 1889 and received its independence 75 years later, in 1964.

Kenyans celebrate their independence from British rule in December 1963.

The African struggle against colonial rule gathered momentum after World War II, inspired by Japanese military successes against the white powers during the war and successful independence struggles in India, Indonesia, and Indochina. By the mid-1950s, colonial rule in Africa had few supporters, and the European powers were preparing to leave. In the decade that followed Ghana's independence in 1957, the British, French, and Belgians withdrew from almost all their African possessions. Only the Portuguese (in Angola, Mozambique, and Portuguese Guinea) and the white minority government of southern Africa clung to colonial power.

Real independence?

"... [there is] nothing but a fancy-dress parade and blare of trumpets. There's nothing save a minimum of readaption, a few reforms at the top, a flag waving: and down there at the bottom an undivided mass, still living in the Middle Ages, endlessly marking time."
Franz Fanon's view of African independence, from his book The Wretched of the Earth, *written in the late 1950s. Fanon was a psychoanalyst and philosopher who wrote about racism and colonial rule. He was concerned that independence alone would not improve the situation of ordinary Africans, especially if the colonial powers did not help them adjust to their new status.*

The dream

In these early years, despite the obvious difficulties that lay ahead, there was a real sense of setting out on a great journey, a sense that Africa could overcome its difficulties and take an equal place in the family of nations. The transition to independence was, with only a few exceptions, relatively peaceful. The new states generally got along with each other. The **Organization of African Unity**, which came into being in 1963, played a useful role in sorting out those disputes that did arise. It also symbolized Africans' determination to take control of their own continent and its destiny.

On the economic front, following the advice of the former **colonial** powers, most African states adopted the same basic plan for development. The main idea was to increase sales to the **developed** countries of whichever product they specialized in—for example, cocoa in Ghana, coffee in Kenya—and to borrow from the developed countries against the profits they expected to make. The money borrowed would be used to diversify the economy (by creating new businesses, both industrial and agricultural) and to improve education, health care, housing, and **infrastructre** (things such as roads, railroads, communication, and electricity). As the new businesses took off, the African country would have more to sell abroad and less need to import goods from other countries. It would become more truly independent and its people would become more prosperous, acquiring higher levels of health, education, and material wealth. That, at least, was the hope and the dream.

There were also good reasons for doubt. These can be divided into political and economic reasons, though in practice the two were often hard to disentangle.

Difficulties—the political inheritance
The politicians who took over the leadership of the newly independent countries were, like politicians everywhere, a mixed bunch. Most had been educated in the West, and many had served in colonial administrations. Their education and lifestyle already set them apart from the great majority of their own people.

In most cases, those involved in the struggle for independence had organized themselves into single political parties. It was these parties that now formed the governments of the new countries. Since there had been no real domestic opposition to independence, there were few opposition parties. The new countries began life without one of the essential ingredients of **democracy**—a real choice between different contenders for government. This stored up problems for the future. One-party states tend to become **dictatorships**, and dictatorships tend to be **corrupt** and inefficient.

In most African countries, the situation was further complicated by **ethnic** issues. At the time of independence, Africa was still a continent of **tribes**—what we would now call ethnic groups—rather than nations. When the Europeans had divided up Africa, they had taken little notice of the existing boundaries between tribes, so most of the "nations" created by the Europeans contained more than one ethnic group. During colonial times the Europeans had often deepened existing hostilities by favoring some groups over others. Those who formed the governments of the newly independent states, and who claimed to speak for the whole nation, often came from a single ethnic group. This created resentment among other groups. When things went badly, they would often blame each other for the failures, and violent conflict would result.

A woman picking coffee beans in Kenya, 1973. The growing of such crops was an important part of plans for development.

Africa's domestic troubles were often made worse by foreign interference. After independence, the **Cold War** between countries following a **free enterprise** system (led by the United States) and those following **communism** (led by the Soviet Union) spread to include Africa. One consequence was that the new African states were sometimes able to play the two countries against each other and use the promise of friendship to win economic aid from one or the other. But overall, the Cold War was a disaster for Africa. If one superpower supported a particular African government, then the other would seek to undermine that government by

Biography – Julius Nyerere

Julius Nyerere (1922–1999) became the first prime minister of independent Tanganyika, in 1961, and the first president of Tanzania (the new nation following the union of Tanganyika and the island state of Zanzibar), in 1964. He was a strong supporter of African culture, and Tanzania became the only country in Africa to have a native tongue, Swahili, as its official language. In politics and economics he championed a form of rural **socialism** called *ujamaa* (literally "familyhood"). It stressed the importance of self-reliance (the ability to make one's own decisions) and Tanzanian independence from the Western economic system. This was largely an economic failure, though it did provide notable improvements in education and health care.

Nyerere did not use power to strut the world stage or enrich himself, and in 1985 he stepped down of his own accord. Though not a saint, he was a man of principle and was much respected throughout the continent.

Julius Nyerere, first president of Tanganyika and Tanzania, and one of Africa's most respected statesmen.

supporting its opponents, who often included both neighboring states and other **ethnic** groups inside the country. This encouragement of national and ethnic hatred was made even more deadly by a growing flood of weapons made in the West and the Soviet Union.

A change of identity: some African states and their new names after independence

Bechuanaland → Botswana
Zaire → Democratic Republic of the Congo
Dahomey → Benin
Northern Rhodesia → Zambia
Nyasaland → Malawi
Southern Rhodesia → Zimbabwe
South-West Africa → Namibia
Tanganyika + Zanzibar → Tanzania

Greenwood Middle School

Difficulties—the economic inheritance

The economic situation was no more promising than the political situation. The **colonial** powers failed to build schools or other training facilities that would provide an educated leadership. The new leaderships had even less experience with economic management than political administration. Most of their people lacked even basic skills such as **literacy**. When independence was given to the four states of French Equatorial Africa (Chad, Central African Republic, Congo-Brazzaville, and Gabon), there were only five university graduates among them. Improving education and creating the sort of health services that a modern workforce required would take money, but no one knew where the money would come from.

The economies of the newly independent countries were not independent. The old systems of **colonial preference**—which forced the **colonies** to sell their products to the colonial power at prices that suited the latter, had disappeared. The new system of global **free enterprise,** however, was not much of an improvement. **Sub-Saharan Africa's** main money earners were minerals (such as copper, gold, and diamonds) and crops grown specifically for the Western market (like coffee and cocoa). The prices paid for these goods, however, were set by the huge Western corporations that controlled distribution and sale, and that could pick and choose where to buy the goods. From the very beginning, the new governments of Africa had almost no control over their own economic destinies.

11

The Muslim/Non-Muslim Divide

Before colonization most Africans followed local, traditional religions. The traders and missionaries brought **Islam** and **Christianity** with them, and many Africans converted (sometimes by force). When the Europeans drew Africa's borders in the late 1800s, they ignored the invisible line dividing the overwhelmingly **Muslim** north of the continent from the non-Muslim south. This line, which snakes across the continent, is not clear-cut, but the states that lie mostly to the south of it, like Ghana or Benin, have a Muslim population of 20 percent or less, while those to the north, like Niger or Mali, have between 80 and 90 percent. To date, there have been no significant Muslim/non-Muslim disputes in these countries. The lasting problems have come in those states that the line cuts roughly in half, for example, Sudan, Nigeria, and, to a lesser extent, Chad.

Sudan

The British ruled Sudan, Africa's largest country, from the end of the 1800s to 1956, but they did not rule it as one country. One administration in Khartoum looked after the **Arab** Muslims of the north (70 percent of the population), while another in Juba looked after the black, mostly Christian, south (30 percent). It was only in the last few years of **colonial** rule that any attempt was made to create a united administration. Almost 50 years after independence, it now seems unfortunate that the attempt was made at all. Whatever the European borders suggested, and the new Muslim Arab government in Khartoum claimed, Sudan was essentially two countries disguised as one.

The new government made little attempt to improve matters, and the military rulers who took over in 1958 only made things worse. The use of the Arabic language was increasingly demanded, Friday rather than Sunday was chosen as the sabbath holiday throughout the country, and Christian missionaries and southern politicians were expelled. In 1963 armed resistance began in the south, led by a group that called itself Anya Nya, or "Snake Venom." Over the next nine years about 400,000 Sudanese lost their lives as a direct result of **civil war.**

In 1972 President Nimeiry made a bold attempt at solving the problem. He told the southern provinces that they would be allowed to rule themselves, that only foreign affairs and defense would be reserved for the central government in Khartoum. But Nimeiry never put his plan into practice, and as the economy declined he became both more **dictatorial** and more aggressively Muslim. In 1983 he tried to impose Muslim **Sharia law** on the whole country. That same year the civil war restarted, this time between the government's army and the south's newly formed Sudan People's Liberation Army. Nineteen years would pass before the next meaningful **cease-fire**.

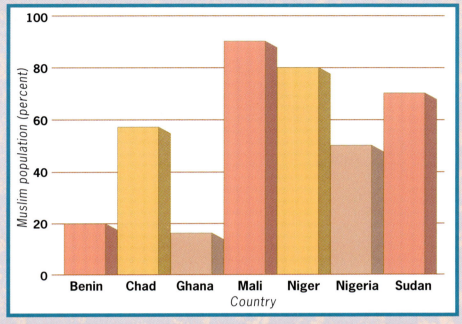

This graph shows the Muslim population (in percentage) in several African countries.

The war continued, but neither side looked capable of winning an outright victory. In the process the south's economy was almost destroyed, and the resulting famines claimed hundreds of thousands of lives. Both sides were guilty of serious breaches of **human rights**, including the sale of captives into slavery. By the time a peace deal was struck in 2002, the overall death toll had probably exceeded 2 million.

Nigeria
Africa's most populous country (approaching 120 million in 2002) is divided almost equally between Muslims and non-Muslims. When the Ibos of the southeast tried to leave Nigeria and create a new state called Biafra, the Yorubas of the southwest joined with the Muslim Hausa of the north to stop them. Once this civil war (1967–1970) was over, great efforts were made to play down tribal differences and strengthen national unity. For most of the

next 30 years the issues dividing **Muslims** and non-Muslims became less important than issues of economic development and administration, as Nigeria seesawed between **military dictatorships** and democratically elected governments.

A Christian church in Kaduna, Nigeria, destroyed by rioting Muslims in February 2000.

However, signs of religious divisions soon reemerged. **Sharia law** was introduced in many of Nigeria's northern states, which many southern Nigerians found threatening. There were several large-scale religious clashes. One in the northern city of Jos in September 2002 claimed more than 500 lives.

Some experts argued that the roots of this violence were economic rather than religious, that simply too many young men in Nigeria were without jobs or prospects. Many of these young men were justifiably angry, and religious extremism gave them the opportunity to express their anger.

Chad

The population of Chad is divided almost equally between the large, thinly populated Muslim north and the small, more thickly populated non-Muslim south. Those from the south, who mostly belong to the Sara **tribe**, were favored by the French **colonial** rulers and inherited the government when independence was granted in 1960. When this government tried to impose its authority on the Muslim tribes of the north, however, the tribes rose in rebellion. By 1968 the situation was so bad that the government invited the French back to restore order. Once this was achieved, the government, rather than seeking reconciliation and real national unity, chose to **persecute** its Muslim citizens. By the mid-1970s the north was once more in open revolt. For the next twelve years the country endured a series of **civil wars** punctuated by occasional **cease-fires** and foreign interventions by France, the United States, and Libya.

During these twelve years, the original dispute between Muslims and non-Muslims was gradually overshadowed by disputes between the different Muslim tribes. It was fighting between these tribes that virtually destroyed the capital N'djamena and set back the country's hopes of economic development. Since 1990 Chad has mostly been at peace, and the recent discovery of significant oil reserves has given the country a chance to break free from the grip of its dismal economic past.

Soldiers of Chad's civil war, July 1984.

Cold War Victims: The Horn of Africa

Between 1947 and 1989, the United States and the Soviet Union competed with each other across the globe in what was known as the **Cold War**. This competition took many forms: political, cultural, economic, military, and scientific. The two sides never actually came to blows with each other—their possession of nuclear weapons made that too dangerous—but they often sought to improve their global position by encouraging their friends and dependents to do so. Sometimes the two **superpowers** tried to use the less developed countries as positive examples of how their own systems worked. But more often than not, they put their energies into undermining each other's dependents. As far as Africa was concerned, their competition was almost completely destructive.

Men, women, and children receive porridge and milk at a relief station in Ethiopia during the famine of 1984–1985.

The Horn of Africa (which is composed of Ethiopia, Eritrea, Somalia, and the small state of Djibouti) interested the superpowers because of its strategic position alongside the

Red Sea oil route from the Middle East to Europe. The United States began supporting Ethiopia (which then included Eritrea) with lavish military aid in 1953, despite the fact that the governing regime of Emperor Haile Selassie was **corrupt** and inefficient. The regime's hatred of **communism** was reason enough for the United States. When neighboring Somalia became independent in 1960, the Soviets offered help and friendship as a way of counteracting U.S. influence in Ethiopia. When the Somali military took power in 1969, the Soviets stepped up this support. They also offered assistance to the Eritreans, who had launched a struggle for independence from Ethiopia in 1961. Each superpower's support was largely military. A region of the world that desperately needed economic assistance was instead overflowing with weaponry.

Swapping sides

In 1974 a single event turned the whole region upside down. The U.S.-supported government in Ethiopia, which had held banquets while 200,000 of its citizens starved in the famine of 1972–1973, was suddenly overthrown by a group of military officers, most of whom had communist sympathies. This group launched a reign of terror against anyone who dared to oppose them. By 1977 one man, Mengistu Haile Mariam, had emerged as the leader of the ruling committee, or Dergue.

By this time, the United States had left, and Ethiopia's enemies had made the most of the Dergue's murderous infighting. Eritrean **guerrillas** had almost evicted the Ethiopians from Eritrea, and Somalia had launched a war to conquer the Ogaden, a vast region of southeastern Ethiopia that the Somalis claimed was theirs. The Dergue asked their fellow communists in the Soviet Union for help. The Soviets, deciding that Ethiopia was a better long-term bet than Somalia or Eritrea, promptly switched allies. Over the next three years, Soviet advisers helped Mengistu retake most of Eritrea and all of the Ogaden. The United States, meanwhile, poured arms into Somalia.

There were many direct casualties of these wars, but many more indirect casualties. Money spent on weapons could not be spent on agricultural development, and resources used to repair war damage could not be used for expansion. The region's economies, already staggering from the effects of the 1970s **world recession**, were brought to their knees by these overlapping wars. The region's ordinary people found their lives becoming harder and more uncertain.

The Live Aid concert at London's Wembley Stadium was held in 1985 to help the victims of the Ethiopian famine.

Music Aid

In October 1984 a British news film about famine in Ethiopia horrified millions of viewers. One of them was Bob Geldof, then the lead singer of the pop group the Boomtown Rats. In November he and Ultravox singer Midge Ure wrote the song "Do They Know It's Christmas?" and recorded it as Band Aid with a large group of British music celebrities. In January 1985 U.S. stars followed suit, joining together as USA for Africa to record "We Are the World." Both these recordings, and the Live Aid concerts in London and Philadelphia, which followed that summer, raised huge sums of money for the charities working to save people from starvation in Ethiopia.

Downward spiral

The region's governments grew more brutal as they struggled to cope. This, in turn, created more violent opposition. By the end of the 1980s, Ethiopia's Mengistu regime was losing its war in Eritrea and facing a formidable military challenge from the Tigray Liberation Front, an army formed in Ethiopia's northernmost province. In 1989 the **Cold War** ended, and the Soviets washed their hands of the regime they had done so much to promote. Two years later the Tigreans drove the Dergue from power, and two years after that Eritrea proclaimed its independence.

Somalia, meanwhile, was falling to pieces. Unlike many African countries it had only one major **ethnic** group, but this was divided into hostile **clans**. In the 1980s, with the country already awash with Soviet and U.S. weapons, the Dergue and its Soviet allies did their best to stir up hatred between these clans. By 1990 **civil war** was raging throughout Somalia, and many towns had been reduced to rubble. As the four major clans fought each other, the central government became increasingly irrelevant and finally nonexistent. **Refugees** poured across the borders in search of food, shelter, and safety. The Somali economy collapsed, leaving famine in its wake.

United Nations troops patrol the streets of the Somali capital Mogadishu in 1992.

In 1992 **United Nations (UN)** troops were sent to maintain order while the famine relief agencies did their job. They suffered serious casualties in violent clashes with the Somali clans. (One of the clashes was turned into a Hollywood film, *Black Hawk Down.*) In 1994, with the famine under control, the UN withdrew its forces, and Somalia returned to chaos. Since then all efforts to create a new central government have failed.

A self-destructive pattern

In 1998 Ethiopia and Eritrea went to war again, this time over a small, disputed strip of virtually worthless land. Eighty-five thousand people were killed, and over half a million refugees fled their homes. A **cease-fire** was signed in July 2000, and both sides agreed to accept the verdict of an independent border commission. In the Horn of Africa the conflicts provoked and encouraged by the Cold War **superpowers** have become almost self-sustaining, a self-destructive pattern that the politicians and soldiers of the region seem unable to break.

Cold War Victims: Angola

The other major African victim of the **Cold War** was Angola. The Portuguese had refused to give up their **colonial** possessions when the other European powers relinquished theirs in the late 1950s and early 1960s, but in 1974 the cost of keeping them provoked a revolution in Portugal itself. The new Portuguese government offered its three colonies a swift transition to independence. In both Portuguese Guinea and Mozambique there was only one major resistance movement to inherit power, but in Angola there were three: the Popular Movement for the Liberation of Angola (MPLA), the National Front for the Liberation of Angola (FLNA), and the National Union for Total Independence of Angola (UNITA). Each was based on a particular **tribe** (the Kimbundu, Bakongo, and Ovimbundu, respectively), and each was supported by one of the **superpowers** (the MPLA by the Soviets, the other two by the United States). The Portuguese tried to persuade them to share power, but failed. As independence and **civil war** loomed, the Soviets and Americans began arming their friends.

First moves

From the beginning the Soviet-supported MPLA controlled the capital, Luanda, and Angola's main source of income, the Cabinda oil wells. This gave it a clear economic advantage. The MPLA also had the more committed, more **idealistic** supporters, which gave it a political and military advantage. By November 1975 the MPLA had effectively destroyed the FNLA and forced the UNITA fighters back into the empty southeast of the huge country. The United States, which had just lost its long war in Vietnam (1965–1975), was reluctant to get involved in a similar conflict in Africa and stopped helping UNITA.

But UNITA was not finished. The white minority government in South Africa, worried that a pro-Soviet government in Angola would threaten both itself and the other white minority regimes in neighboring Southern Rhodesia and South-West Africa (later Zimbabwe and Namibia), came to the rescue. They offered the UNITA leader Jonas Savimbi all the financial and military help he needed to keep the war going.

War by proxy

For the first ten years, until about 1987, UNITA's campaign was more of an annoyance than a threat to President dos Santos's MPLA government. The Soviets offered some economic help,

Cuban troops helped train the army, and the government pushed ahead with its **communist** program. Its education and health care reforms were much-needed and popular, but the government's method of copying inappropriate Soviet economic policies—taking many banks, industries, and farms into state ownership—was inefficient. Ultimately this deprived the country of the money it needed to pay for the education and health care programs. As the war with UNITA continued, eating up money on arms and deterring foreign investors, the government became increasingly dependent on Angola's oil wealth to keep itself afloat.

UNITA had few real supporters. Savimbi's organization was a brutal **dictatorship** that condemned women opponents as witches and burned them alive. It raised some of the money it needed by selling Angola's diamonds on the international market, but mostly relied on the financial help that it received from the South Africans and, eventually, the Americans. By the mid-1980s the Reagan administration in Washington was smelling victory in the Cold War and was eager to take on the Soviets wherever it found them.

UNITA leader Jonas Savimbi shares a song with some of his troops at a station on Angola's Benguela Railway, April 1986.

By 1987 the war was turning in UNITA's favor, and more Cuban troops were needed to stem the tide. This upsurge in fighting did more damage to the economy, and the end of the **Cold War** in 1990 meant that the MPLA would soon have to survive without Soviet and Cuban help. Fortunately for the MPLA, South Africa was also under pressure to withdraw from the conflict, and in 1991 an agreement was reached. Both the Cubans and the South Africans would leave Angola, and nationwide elections would be held under **UN** supervision. Both Savimbi and the Americans were confident that UNITA would win the election—the Ovimbundu were, after all, Angola's largest **tribe**—but they didn't take into consideration Savimbi's reputation for brutality and the fact that many Angolans blamed him for the length of the war. In September 1992 the MPLA won a majority in the assembly, and dos Santos beat Savimbi for the presidency.

"Blood diamonds"

Over half the world's diamonds are found in Africa. Control of their excavation and sale has become a key element in many of Africa's most crippling wars. Easy to transport, hard to trace, and simple to convert into cash, diamonds have become the most popular way of paying for the soldiers and weaponry that have terrorized countries like Angola, Liberia, Sierra Leone, and the Congo. Just as money paid out for killings has earned the name "blood money," so the diamonds used to finance Africa's wars have become known as "blood diamonds."

The final chapter

The United States admitted that the elections had been "generally free and fair," but Savimbi refused to recognize the result. In October 1992 he tried and failed to seize power through a **coup**, and in January 1993 he restarted the **civil war.** Towns throughout the country were besieged by UNITA forces, and the war entered its most terrible phase. By mid-1993 more than 1,000 people a day were dying in battles or sieges or from the famine spread by war. Between 10 and 15 million land mines had been sown across the country, and 100,000 Angolans had already lost at least one limb. *The New York Times* reporter John Darnton discovered one small town where 20,000 people, half of them children, were living on a diet of boiled insects and leaves.

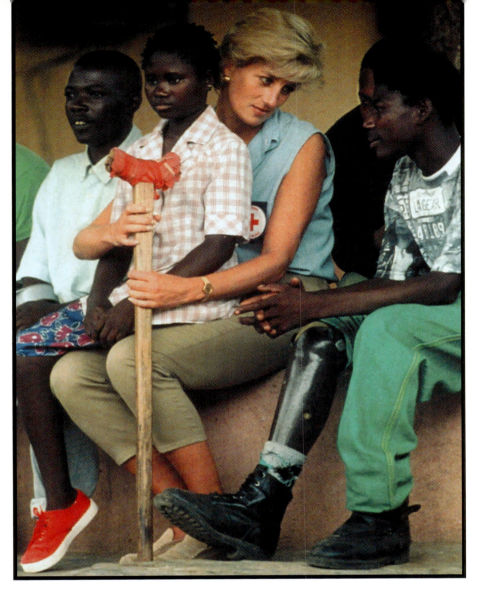

Britain's Princess Diana talks to Angolan victims of land mines at an orthopedic workshop in Luanda, 1997.

In 1994 the tide turned in favor of the MPLA government, and Savimbi would never again come so close to victory. He had lost his American backers. Now that the Cold War was over, Washington had drastically reduced its interest in African affairs. In 1995 Savimbi accepted the role of vice president in a unified government, but then failed to turn up when the government was sworn in. In 1998 he once again restarted the war and the violence continued until a peace deal was finally struck in 2002. Savimbi himself was killed in February 2002.

Thieves and Murderers

The legacies of slavery and colonialism, the harsh economic realities imposed by Western corporations and financial institutions, and the destructive impact of the **Cold War** all made life difficult for most African countries and their governments. But these governments were not completely powerless. They usually had some money to spend and the chance to borrow more. A few African governments did their best to use what resources they possessed for the good of all their people: Tanzania under Julius Nyerere was a good example. Most African governments said they wanted to help their own people, but many were just as interested in enriching themselves. A small number went even further, abandoning all responsibility for the welfare of the people they ruled and helping themselves to whatever they could. These governments looted their own countries and murdered anyone foolish or courageous enough to object.

Idi Amin is sworn in as Uganda's new head of state in February 1971. During his eight years in power, he tortured and murdered thousands of political opponents.

Idi Amin

Independent Uganda's first leader was Milton Obote. His nine years in office were marked by increasing heavy-handedness, economic inefficiency, and tribal favoritism. In January 1971 he was overthrown by the head of the country's armed forces, Major-General Idi Amin Dada. Amin strengthened his position by killing those soldiers who came from **tribes** and Ugandan regions other than his own, and by employing large numbers of mercenaries (soldiers for hire) from neighboring countries. He and his new army spent the next eight years plundering the country and killing anyone who opposed them.

Cashing in on power

During Idi Amin's rule in Uganda, planes loaded with luxury goods for Amin and his supporters—cars, jewelry, audio and video equipment—frequently left England's Stansted Airport for the Ugandan capital, Kampala. The regularity of these flights earned them a nickname—"The Stansted Shuttle."

In 1972 Amin expelled all South Asians who had settled in Uganda during the period of British **colonial** rule. He divided their property and contracts among his supporters. Since the supporters had no experience of running such businesses, most of them collapsed, and by 1978 the country's economy had shrunk to half its former size. Amin also set up a notorious security and intelligence force called the State Research Bureau. This force tortured and murdered as many as half a million Ugandans. Most were ordinary people, but Amin's victims included ministers, archbishops, and even his own wife.

In September 1978 Amin made the mistake of attacking neighboring Tanzania, probably with the intention of distracting his own people's attention from their economic problems. The Tanzanians pushed Amin's army back across the border and reached the Uganda capital of Kampala in the spring of 1979. Amin fled abroad, but many of his supporters retreated into the more inaccessible regions of the Ugandan countryside and continued their reign of terror.

Obote returned to power but repeated his earlier mistakes. In 1986 he was replaced by Yoweni Museveni, who began the daunting process of repairing and restoring those parts of the country that the central government controlled. He made much progress over the next sixteen years, but rebellions continued in the north and west, now led by the so-called Lord's Resistance Army. This group claimed to follow the Ten Commandments, but specialized in kidnapping young girls for its leaders.

Joseph Mobutu in 1961, before he became president of the Congo.

Mobutu

When the Belgian Congo was granted independence in 1960 there were great hopes for the new country's future. Although the Belgians had done nothing to prepare the country for independence, there were huge reserves of cobalt, diamonds, and copper. New hydroelectric dams on the Congo River had the potential to supply all the energy central Africa needed. Yet by the end of the century, the country was deep in debt, its **infrastructure** in complete disrepair. Disease was rampant, unemployment running at 60 percent, and **inflation** at 30 percent. The economy had been failing for the last 20 years.

The responsibility for this state of affairs rested with one man. Mobutu Sese Seko liked to call himself "Papa," or the nation's "Founder and Guide." He came to power in 1965, after five years of intervention by **Cold War** rivals had worsened existing tribal animosities and destroyed any chances of a government that represented all the people. Mobutu attacked the colonial past and encouraged pride in African heritage. He changed his name from Joseph Mobutu to Mobutu Seso Seko and renamed the country Zaire, replacing European city and town names with African ones. He imprisoned or executed his enemies and installed his friends in power. He denounced **communism** at every opportunity, which kept him on good terms with the United States and France. Both countries sent forces to save him from his own people in the late 1970s.

The country earned money from the sale of its minerals and received substantial loans and aid from Western financial institutions. Mobutu and his friends pocketed most of it. The dictator had luxury homes in several European countries and many Congolese provinces; he traveled the world with a huge entourage, staying at the best hotels and shopping at the most exclusive stores. Billions of dollars were hidden away in Swiss bank accounts. Mobutu's regime even gave rise to a new word. Just as people with a compulsion to steal are known as kleptomaniacs, regimes that seem unable to stop looting their own countries are now called "kleptocracies."

Bokassa

In 1966 the Central African Republic was taken over by its army leader, Jean-Bedel Bokassa. He declared himself president-for-life and then proclaimed himself emperor of the new "Central African Empire." During his fourteen years in power, he treated the whole country as if it were his personal property. Bokassa filled his luxurious palace with gold and diamonds and killed whomever he felt like killing. Some enemies were dropped in the Ubangi River for the crocodiles; others were reportedly cooked and served up to visiting foreigners. His coronation ceremony, modeled on Napoleon's in 1804, cost the country everything it earned from export sales in a whole year. French governments supported him for years, but they finally decided he had gone too far when many children were clubbed to death in 1979. French forces overthrew him, and his successors put him on trial. A death sentence was reduced to life imprisonment. Bokassa eventually died in 1996. The Central African Republic is still struggling to recover from his years in power.

Jean-Bedel Bokassa, the self-styled emperor of Central Africa, at his coronation in 1977.

Turning Point: 1970s—Oil Prices Rise

The conflicts discussed in previous pages all took place in the 1960s or early 1970s, when the rest of the African continent was still under the friendlier influence of postindependence optimism. Many of the new African governments managed to stay out of the **Cold War** and cope with the **tribal** and/or religious tensions that afflicted their countries. They prevented the concentration of power in the hands of brutal dictators and their supporters. For most of these governments, the development strategy of increasing exports and borrowing to fund a growing, more diversified economy seemed to be working. An average growth rate of about 3 percent was achieved in the 1960s. Though far from high, this seemed a good first step on the road to development. Africa and its politicians had come some way toward meeting the expectations of independence.

New oil pipelines in Nigeria, October 1965. The country's huge oil reserves have played a vital role in keeping the economy afloat.

African countries are hit hard

By the end of the 1970s, these hopes had been dashed. In 1973, and again in 1979, the price of crude oil soared, raising the cost of a barrel. The causes of this price explosion had nothing to do with Africa, but its effects were a particular disaster for the continent. Only a handful of countries in **sub-Saharan African** had energy supplies of their own, and the rest relied on imported oil for between 60 and 90 percent of their energy needs. Development plans designed around cheap oil now had to be rewritten. Each extra dollar spent on imported oil was one dollar less to invest in the future.

There was more bad news. In the **developed** West, higher oil prices made industrial goods more expensive to produce and transport, so African countries found they were paying more for these, too. At the same time, the world economic slowdown that followed the oil price rises meant that the Western economies wanted less of the raw materials that Africa sold. The price of these went down. African governments were hit both ways. As less money flowed in, more flowed out.

Three other factors played a part in making things even worse. The spread of Western medical knowledge was one of colonialism's more welcome contributions to Africa, but even this had its downside. Thanks to better health care, the population was now growing at over 3 percent per year. Food production, on the other hand, was not growing at the same speed. Most of the newly independent governments had made a point of encouraging their farmers to grow crops for export, not for food. They had also welcomed the drift to the towns, thinking that the new industries and services would need workers, but overlooking the fact that those workers also needed food. By the 1980s many African countries were spending more and more of their diminishing income on importing food that they could have grown themselves.

Terms of trade

*"Throughout Africa the story is the same. Africa is in debt. Because it must reduce spending, it cannot build up its **infrastructure** to compete with industrialized nations. It cannot control the price paid for its exports, which keep falling. It cannot determine the price it pays for goods it must import, which keep rising. It wants fair trade.... In theory, Africa is free to trade: in practice, it faces immense problems."*
From Africa in Crisis, *an educational pack put together by* **the Save the Children organization**

Finally, there was a growing problem of debt. As governments found it harder and harder to balance their budgets, so they began to borrow more and more. Year by year the interest on the loans increased. By 1982 Mobutu's Zaire needed two-thirds of its annual income just to pay the interest on that year's debt and what was still owed from the previous year.

Unhelpful aid

By the 1980s Africa was in dire need of economic help, but little meaningful assistance was given. Western people gave generously in crisis situations like the Ethiopian famine of 1984–1985, but their governments were not as helpful. They gave the Africans weapons and money that had to be spent on goods from their own countries, even when these goods could be bought more cheaply elsewhere. Such aid tended to be more profitable for the giver than the receiver.

A father and his two children at the Korem aid center in Ethiopia during the famine of 1984–1985.

The international institutions that had been set up by the **UN**—the International Bank for Reconstruction and Development (the World Bank) and the International Monetary Fund (the IMF)—were prepared to lend the Africans more money, but only on terms acceptable to the Western countries that supplied the funds. African countries were asked to stop subsidizing food prices for their poor and to reduce health and education services that their economies could not really afford. They were also told to "free up" their economies, which meant removing any health and safety restrictions, or any **trade union** powers to protect wages, that might deter Western companies from investing in their countries.

Economic inequality within Africa becomes even more severe in times of crisis. While some maintain a relatively high standard of living, hundreds of thousands, like these Kenyans in Nairobi, live in poverty.

These conditions were bound to further impoverish ordinary Africans and to widen the gap between them and the elites who ruled them. Some African officials, less concerned with their people's well-being than the maintenance of their own privileged lifestyles, accepted the conditions willingly. Others did so with considerable reluctance. But most gave in.

Things fall apart

This change of economic direction had obvious political consequences. Ordinary Africans noticed that their rulers continued to live well while their own lives got harder and harder, and they grew increasingly angry. Their expectations of independence were no longer being met, and their own governments seemed at least partly to blame. These African governments were within reach, unlike the foreign governments and corporations that made so many of the decisions that affected African lives.

Many of the governments sought to deflect their people's anger onto others. Unable to blame their Western backers, these governments sought out people to blame at home, often picking on the representatives of other **tribes**. These tribes fought back, and incidents of violence multiplied. As Africa's economy shrank, more than a few of its nations began to unravel.

31

West African Civil Wars

During the 1990s two West African states were virtually destroyed by horrible **civil wars.** These two conflicts, in Liberia and Sierra Leone, had very similar causes and followed remarkably similar paths. As such, they offered a vivid and frightening picture of where much of Africa was heading if the continent's economy were allowed to collapse.

Master-Sergeant Samuel K. Doe seized the presidency of Liberia in 1980.

End of a regime

The event that triggered civil war in Liberia was a government attempt, in April 1979, to raise the price of rice—which formed a large part of most ordinary Liberians' diet—by 50 percent. Massive riots were followed by harsh repression and a military **coup**. In April 1980 the group that had ruled Liberia for a century and a half was overthrown by seventeen low-ranking soldiers led by Master-Sergeant Samuel K. Doe. All the old government leaders were executed. Thirteen of them were tied to posts on the beach and shot in front of television news cameras. Free elections, a new **constitution,** and economic justice were promised. None were delivered.

The only real difference between the new regime and the old was that a different tribal group was now in power. Members of Doe's **tribe**—the Krahns—were given all the important posts; any outspoken opponents were imprisoned and, more often than not, tortured and killed. The regime lived off the sale of diamonds and its share of the U.S.-owned Firestone Rubber Corporation's profits. The rest of the economy, and the living standards of ordinary Liberians, were allowed to collapse.

Death of a country

On Christmas Eve of 1989, an army led by Charles Taylor invaded the country from bases in neighboring Guinea. His troops were mostly from the Gio and Mano tribes, who together made up about a sixth of Liberia's population. Many were still children, and they were often given alcohol or drugs to make them less afraid. Over the next eight months Taylor's troops burned, raped, and murdered their way across the country, reducing Doe's soldiers to a foothold on the coast and encouraging the birth of other armies representing other tribes.

In August 1990 a West African Multilateral Force involving troops from Nigeria, Ghana, Guinea, Sierra Leone, and The Gambia tried to restore order and failed. Doe died at the hands of one rebel army, but no one was able to gain complete control of the country. For the next seven years Liberia and its people were ravaged by up to six tribally based armies, each intent on wiping out their tribal enemies. By 1994 over 5 percent of the population had been killed.

The other West African states continued with their efforts, and these, along with a general war-weariness, finally led to elections in July 1997. These were won by Charles Taylor, mostly because Liberians knew he would start the war again if he lost. For two years there was relative peace, but a new rebellion began in 1999. By 2002 Taylor's rule was under serious threat. Liberia, like Somalia, had become virtually ungovernable.

Child soldiers

At the end of the 1990s there were approximately 300,000 soldiers, operating in 30 countries, who were under the age of 18. Modern weapons are light and easy to operate, thus encouraging the recruitment of children—often forced—in many wars. Since 1994 the UN has been trying to create new international rules forbidding the recruitment of child soldiers.

"I joined when I was thirteen years old. I was forced to fight because I was separated from my parents and the rest of my family. I had to fight for my own survival. I was given six months of training and became a special forces member. I fought on the front lines, but I wasn't afraid the first time because I had been given drugs. I fired a mortar. I experienced some terrible things during the war. I saw some terrible things and did some terrible things. I saw people being killed, I saw fighters eat people's hearts. They burned people and killed babies. I did these things too because we had to obey orders. After the war, I tried to find my family, but they have disappeared. So now I live near a roadside store. That's where I live and sleep. I am haunted by what we did during the war.... I have lost my ability to feel. You can cut me with a knife and I won't even feel it. I cry but only when I'm happy."

A child soldier from Liberia, from the Radio Netherlands Human Rights Internet site. (In 1997 this boy was given a place in a carpentry class, where he learned how to make furniture.)

Liberians flee from their country's civil war on a Nigerian cargo ship, May 1996.

Repeat prescription

The **civil war** in Sierra Leone began in 1991, two years after the beginning of civil war in Liberia. As in Liberia, there was massive dissatisfaction among the population as a whole. Falling world prices for agricultural products and the inefficiency of local politicians had led to a dramatic decline in ordinary living standards, but those same local politicians continued to prosper, thanks to their control of the country's diamond, bauxite, and titanium mines. In March 1991 a group calling itself the Revolutionary United Front (RUF) began an armed rebellion. Three years of butchery and destruction later, the RUF and its leader Foday Sankoh were in control of the country's mines.

The weakened central government was overthrown by a military **coup,** elections were held, and the winner was overthrown by another coup. Several armies were now fighting each other, and another West African Multilateral Force was sent in. The elected government was reinstated, but lasted less than a year. In early 1999 RUF soldiers took over Freetown, maiming and murdering thousands of women, children, and old people. Much of the city was burned down. By this time the country's economy had collapsed, and half the country's people had fled their homes. By 2000, however, Foday Sankoh had been captured, and a permanent settlement seemed to be developing.

Turning Point: Genocide in Rwanda

The **genocide** in Rwanda had roots in both **colonial** history and the economic crisis of the 1980s, but it was committed by Africans against Africans. The initial crime against humanity was terrible enough in itself, but it also triggered a wider war in central Africa that eventually involved half a dozen other African states and may have cost as many as 3 million lives.

The power of hatred

Rwanda is a small, fertile country with a large population; 90 percent are Hutus, the other 10 percent are mostly Tutsis. The two peoples share the same language and much of the same culture, but they have long been traditional enemies, both in Rwanda and in neighboring Burundi. The Belgian colonial rulers reinforced this hostility by favoring the Tutsis at the Hutus' expense, giving them the best administrative jobs and business contracts.

After independence the Hutus took power, and there was massive discrimination against the once-dominant Tutsis, many of whom moved to neighboring Uganda, Burundi, and Zaire. In 1990 these Tutsi exiles, who numbered well over half a million, formed their own army, the Rwandese Patriotic Front (RPF), with the intention of eventually returning to reclaim their lost lands and rights. The Hutu government in Rwanda, led by President Juvénal Habyarimana, expanded its own army with French help. All-out war between the two **tribes** seemed imminent.

By this time the Rwandan economy, like most African economies, was in bad shape. Coffee exports supplied 75 percent of the country's income, and the price of coffee on the world market had collapsed. The country's population, meanwhile, had grown at a rapid rate. There were more mouths to feed, but less money to buy food.

The international community was willing to help Rwanda, but only if the government sorted out the tribal conflict that was threatening to tear the country apart. Habyarimana agreed in principle to multiparty elections and the merging of his Hutu army with the Tutsi RPF, but his own supporters prevented him from keeping these promises. He was returning to the Rwandan capital of Kigali on April 6, 1994, when his plane was shot down, almost certainly by his former supporters in the *interahamwe*, the semiofficial Hutu militia whose name means "those who stand together." For them, fear and hatred of the Tutsis were more important than Rwanda's economic well-being.

Genocide

Before the assassination was even announced on the radio, the *interahamwe* squads had begun killing Habyarimana's Hutu supporters and any Tutsis they could find. Fictional reports of Tutsi attacks were broadcast on the state radio, and Hutus were told to defend themselves. At the same time, orders were passed down through government channels for the mass murder of the Tutsis. The authorities in each town and village were told that only the complete elimination of the Tutsis—men, women, children, and babies—would guarantee their own safety. These authorities handed out weapons and told their people where to find the Tutsis. Any who protested were themselves threatened or killed.

The bodies of Tutsis, massacred by Hutus, lie outside a Rwandan church, 1994.

The terrified Tutsis ran for their lives, but few escaped. Those who sought sanctuary in churches or hospitals were either dragged out and killed or burned to death inside the buildings. Over the next hundred days about a million Tutsis were murdered by Hutu armed groups and mobs.

Terror

"Our sector was attacked on the night of the 10th [April]. We watched as our houses were burned down and our cows stolen and eaten.... [We fled] toward the Adventist church of Muhomboli....

"On the 13th, we saw an enormous group of militia.... They surrounded the church.... They threw grenades through the windows and doors that they managed to break down. Once they overcame all resistance from the refugees they entered the church. I saw that death was waiting for me. I pretended to be dead and listened to the movement of the killers as I lay underneath many corpses."
Justin Kanamugire, a 32-year-old Tutsi farmer, quoted in African Rights, Rwanda: Death, Despair and Defiance

Aftermath

The Tutsi RPF invaded from Uganda, and by early July had captured Kigali. As the Tutsi troops fanned out across the country, more than a million Hutus fled westward, over the Zairean border.

UN troops evacuate Hutu survivors of a massacre committed by the (mostly Tutsi) Rwandan Army, April 1995.

Inside Rwanda a government was set up that included both Tutsis and Hutus, and order was slowly restored. The United States, still stinging from its failure in Somalia, refused to sanction the sending of a **UN** peacekeeping force, but French troops created a **safety zone** in southwest Rwanda for those Hutus who wished to return.

Rwandan refugees on the march in November 1996.

The **refugee** camps across the Zairean border were over-crowded, unsanitary, and poorly supplied. These camps were home to the worst of the *interahamwe* killers, who over the next few years would usually be called the **genocidaires**. Few were in favor of helping such men, but they had guns, so they ran the camps. As aid poured in from the international relief agencies, the Hutu genocidaires recovered their strength. Within a year they were ready to threaten the peace once more, in both their old home of Rwanda and their new home, Mobutu's Congo.

Seeking justice

Late in 1994 a UN tribunal was set up in Arusha, Tanzania, to try those suspected of playing a leading role in the Rwandan genocide. Many of the wanted men were hard to find, evidence was often difficult to obtain and confirm, and progress was extremely slow. By 2000 only seven verdicts had been handed down by the UN-appointed judges. Since then, several more suspects have been flushed out of their European and U.S. hiding places and sent back to Arusha, but it seems unlikely that the principal authors and perpetrators of the **genocide** will ever stand trial.

Africa's "Great War"

The **genocidaires** who dominated the **refugee** camps in eastern Zaire had no intention of spending their whole lives as refugees. Through 1995 and early 1996, they conducted military raids across the Rwandan border, built up their supply of weapons, and sought allies for an eventual reconquest of their homeland. The Zairean government, which was fighting rebellious Tutsis on its own territory and Ugandan rebels based in eastern Zaire, supported the genocidaires.

Fearing an invasion, the new Tutsi-dominated government in Rwanda formed alliances of its own: with Tutsi rebels in eastern Zaire, the Ugandan government, and Zairean rebels led by Laurent Kabila. The Tutsi government initially restricted themselves to arming and supporting these partners inside Zaire, but in October 1996 it took the final plunge and launched a full-scale invasion. Within days the refugee camps had been cleared. Some 700,000 Hutus fled back across the border to Rwanda; a further 400,000—which included most of the genocidaires—retreated westward into the vast rain forests of Zaire. Rwanda's domestic nightmare had now become a war between the Tutsis and Kabila on the one side, and the Hutu genocidaires and Mobutu on the other.

Rebel leader Laurent Kabila addresses some of his troops in February 1997. He became president of Zaire in May 1997.

The next phase of the conflict proved shorter than most observers expected. Most of Mobutu's forces ran away from the invaders, looting villages and killing civilians as they fled. By May 1997 the Rwandan-supported rebels were approaching the Zairean capital of Kinshasa. Mobutu escaped to Morocco, only to die of cancer soon afterward. Laurent Kabila, who had been fighting him for over 30 years, took over the government. Zaire was renamed the Democratic Republic of the Congo.

It soon became apparent that Kabila was not much of an improvement on his predecessor. He snuffed out hopes of international help for his poverty-stricken country by insulting foreign diplomats and holding foreign businesspeople for ransom. Rather than take sensible action to help the economy, he simply printed more money and made the situation worse. He also failed to reward his Rwandan backers by handing over the Hutu genocidaires. On the contrary, he employed them to protect his own government. Throughout those areas of the newly named Congo that he controlled, Kabila behaved as **dictatorially** as Mobutu had done.

"It's our country"

"In Walungu Hospital, near Bukavu, 1,200 patients compete for 300 beds, and the attention of three doctors. About half the inmates are relatively healthy, but too terrified to go back home. Murals in the hospital depict black doctors in white coats peering into microscopes, recalling the lost hopes of the 1960s. Now, the wards are full of black children with blond hair, a sign of malnutrition. The hospital's head of nursing says she has received only three months' salary in her whole career. Why does she carry on? 'It's our country,' she shrugs. 'It's painful, but there it is.'"
Quoted in "Africa's Great War," The Economist, July 6, 2002.

Kabila had supporters. The MPLA government in neighboring Angola had never gotten along with Mobutu, because Mobutu had allowed UNITA to use Zairean territory as a safe base. Kabila, on the other hand, was more than willing to sacrifice UNITA in return for Angolan government support. The government of Robert Mugabe in Zimbabwe and Sam Nujoma's government in Namibia also offered military help. Their motives were mixed: sympathy with Kabila, a distraction from domestic troubles, and greed for the Congo's mineral riches.

Congolese rebel forces head for the capital, Kinshasa, in August 1998, intent on overthrowing President Kabila.

Kabila's supporters, however, were no match for his enemies. Within a year of his installation as president, he had lost the eastern half of the Congo to various rebel armies supported by the Rwandans and Ugandans. In 1998 Rwanda sent its own 40,000-strong army—the best-organized fighting force in Central Africa—across the border once more. The intention, as before, was to destroy the genocidaires and their Congolese protector. In 1996 the protector had been Mobutu. Now it was Kabila.

The "Great War"
The Congo is a vast, heavily forested country with few paved roads, few working telephones, and many **tribes**. For one state to permanently restrain it was next to impossible, particularly when other states were eager to enter the dispute. Uganda offered the Rwandans support in the east; Angola and Zimbabwe sent forces to protect Kabila in the west. Namibia, Chad, and Burundi also sent some troops to help one side or the other, if only briefly. The troubles of Rwanda had merged with the troubles of the Congo, and the troubles of the Congo had turned into what journalists began calling Africa's "Great War."

This term was somewhat misleading. Over the next four years the Congo was consumed by many loosely connected minor wars, not one great battle between competing alliances. What little law and order still existed simply disintegrated, leaving the ordinary people at the mercy of whichever armed groups happened to be in the neighborhood. The country was stripped bare. Hundreds of thousands of people were killed, many by soldiers, many more by the famine that followed.

There was no chance of anyone winning this war but many chances to make a profit. The original motivation behind the various foreign incursions was varied. The Rwandan government had reason to dislike Kabila's support for the fugitive Hutus, and the Ugandans had similar concerns about Ugandan rebels using northeastern Congo as a safe haven. The Angolan government was grateful to Kabila for shutting out UNITA and feared that a different Congolese government might let them back in. Kabila himself asked the Zimbabweans for military protection.

The Zimbabweans agreed, but only in return for a share of Congolese diamond and cobalt profits. The greed of the other states involved was not so obvious at first, but as the war ground to a stalemate it became increasingly clear that all of them were effectively looting the country. One **UN** report criticized Uganda, Zimbabwe, and Burundi for illegally exporting Congolese diamonds, copper, coltan, cobalt, and gold. Another report listed some 30 Western companies that had conspired with them. As the 20th century ended, the Congo's wealth was disappearing and its people were living in terror.

Congolese take the town of Sona Bata, 40 miles (65 kilometers) from Kinshasa, August 1998.

Independence: 40 Years Later

The violence and heart-wrenching misery that afflicted Somalia, Angola, Liberia, Sierra Leone, and the Congo in the 1990s stole most of the headlines in world news. But there were 35 other states in **sub-Saharan Africa**, and most of these were struggling with similar problems. Unlike the five states listed above, they had not, as yet, been overwhelmed by their problems. But neither had they solved them.

Politics
The end of the **Cold War** had both positive and negative impacts on Africa. On the positive side, African states were no longer subject to **superpower** manipulation and interference. If one **tribe** was in power in a pro-Western country, the other tribes were not being stirred up and armed by the Soviets, and vice versa. On the negative side, countries were no longer being bribed with economic help to keep them loyal. The Africans had lost their chance to play one side against the other. More seriously, the continent had become less important to the rest of the world.

One positive consequence was the spread of **democracy** that took place in the 1990s. At the beginning of that decade, multiparty systems only existed in Botswana, The Gambia, Senegal, Zimbabwe, and Namibia. Once the Cold War was over, many Western governments and financial institutions started demanding moves toward democracy as a condition for giving aid. There was self-interest in this—democratic states tended to be more stable and therefore offered greater security for Western investments—but it also made many African governments more accountable to their own people.

These political improvements were patchy and sometimes canceled out by a steady weakening of social values. In many countries 40 years of **corrupt** government had removed all respect for politicians and the law, and the stressing of tribal identities had reduced any sense of nationhood or wider humanity. The flood of **refugees** fleeing the continent's many wars had stretched African life-support systems to the limit. Ordinary people had grown used to doing whatever they needed to do, and taking whatever they needed to take, in order to survive. In the sprawling **shanty towns** that ringed Africa's cities, crime was rampant.

Global warming

Over the last 30 years, Africa has suffered from unusually severe climatic conditions. Drought struck at the Sahel (a region with little rainfall to the south of the Sahara) throughout the 1970s and 1980s, in Ethiopia, Somalia, and Sudan at frequent intervals in the 1980s and 1990s, and in southern Africa in the early 1990s. By contrast, Mozambique and Malawi faced torrential rains and widespread flooding in 2000–2001. Most experts believe that **global warming**—which is mostly caused by the burning of fossil fuels like oil and coal—has been responsible for these increasingly violent shifts in normal climactic patterns. Those same experts agree that the less **developed** countries will find it much harder to cope with the consequences of global warming, so Africa is likely to suffer more than most. Africans, of course, are quick to point out that global warming has, for the most part, been caused by the industries of the developed world.

Mozambicans in February 2000, trapped by rising floodwaters.

AIDS

By the end of the 20th century HIV/AIDS had infected more than 25 million people in **sub-Saharan Africa.** In the year 2000 alone, 10,500 new cases were reported each day. This rapid spread of the virus, while obviously tragic for each and every victim, also threatened the whole economic future of the region.

Since HIV/AIDS is sometimes transmitted by sex, the portion of the population most at risk is that aged 15–45, the same portion responsible for building the economy. The World Bank announced in 2000 that the epidemic was at least partly to blame for the decline in Africa's already poor growth rate. If the disease is not quickly brought under control—something that at present seems highly unlikely—the continent seems to be heading for a human and economic catastrophe.

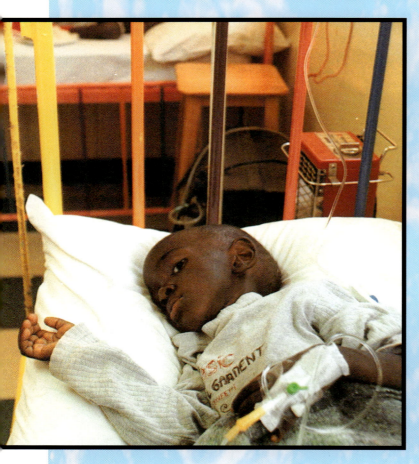

John Githinji Paul, a three-year-old with HIV/AIDS, rests in his bed at a home for AIDS orphans in Nairobi, Kenya, 2000.

Economics

The end of the **Cold War** had little impact on Africa's economic situation. The decline of the late 1970s and 1980s continued into the 1990s. Held down by debt, Western self-interest, and the **corruption** of their own governments, only 4 of sub-Saharan Africa's 40 states managed a better than 2 percent growth rate —the sort of rate all European and North American countries took for granted—in the years 1987–1997. The economies of 22 sub-Saharan states shrank rather than grew. Africa was sliding backward.

The West African state of Ghana offered a good example of how things were going wrong. There was no **civil war** in Ghana, and the government during this period, though hardly democratic in the Western sense, was neither brutal nor particularly **corrupt**. Through the 1990s the country seemed to be making modest but steady progress. But in 2000 its economy was hit by a drastic fall in the world price of cocoa (one of its two main exports), an unusually low price for gold (the other chief export), and a twofold increase in the price of its oil imports. There was nothing the Ghanaian government could do about this, other than hope for a change in its economic circumstances.

Africa was given notice of one welcome change in 1999. The Western governments, awash with the wealth amassed during a decade of excellent economic growth, announced that they were canceling at least some of the debt owed by some African countries. The list of countries was expanded in both 2000 and 2001, and these **debt relief** measures were certainly welcomed by many African governments and peoples. They were, however, often less generous than they seemed and in themselves did little to solve the basic problems afflicting the African economy. The West, while insisting that only **free enterprise** could help Africa, protected its own agriculture against African competition. What Africa needed was the opposite, permission to protect its own infant industries, and unrestricted access to Western markets.

Three Leaders

Since independence there has been a bewildering variety of African leaders. Many of them have had both a positive and negative influence on their countries.

Jerry Rawlings: Ghana

Born in Accra, Ghana, in 1947, Jerry Rawlings became an officer in Ghana's postindependence air force. In June 1979 he led the group of junior officers that overthrew the last in a succession of **corrupt** military governments. After jailing or executing those he considered responsible for the **corruption**, Rawlings returned the country to civilian rule. Two years later, deciding that nothing had really changed, he seized power again. The **constitution** was suspended, political parties banned, and measures introduced to increase the participation of ordinary Ghanaians in economic and political decision-making. The country's poor economic performance—mostly caused by Ghana's international situation but not helped by Rawlings' policies—eventually forced a change of direction. An economic recovery program was accepted with the IMF and World Bank, and **democracy** was slowly reintroduced. Rawlings won presidential elections in both 1992 and 1996 before stepping down in 2000. Critics stressed his poor **human rights** record, while supporters argued that his rule had saved Ghana from corruption and serious tribal strife.

Jerry Rawlings

Daniel arap Moi: Kenya

A member of Kenya's Kalenjin **ethnic** minority, Daniel arap Moi was born in 1924. He was appointed vice president by Jomo Kenyatta, Kenya's first postindependence leader, in 1967. When Kenyatta died in 1978, Moi became president, a post he held until 2002. Like many African leaders, he changed the

Daniel arap Moi

political system to secure his position and increase his power, surrounded himself with members of his own **tribe** and helped himself to the nation's wealth. When corrupt and inefficient management worsened the country's existing economic problems, he sought to divert attention from his own failures by stirring up grievances between tribes. In the 1990s international and domestic pressure forced Moi to reintroduce democratic elections; in both 1992 and 1997 he triumphed over a tribally divided opposition. However, the country's constitution forbade him from running again in the December 2002 elections. His chosen successor for the presidency, Jomo Kenyatta's son Uhuru, was soundly beaten. It remains to be seen whether the new president, Mwai Kibaki, whose supporters include many former supporters of Moi, will introduce any real economic and political changes.

Olusegun Obasanjo: Nigeria

This Nigerian leader was born in 1937. A career soldier from the Yoruba tribe, Obasanjo headed the military government that took power in 1976. Three years later he became the first African military leader to hand power back to civilians, as he announced his retirement from politics. He was still considered a threat, however, and in 1995 he was imprisoned by the **dictatorial** Sani Abacha. When Abacha died in 1998, Obasanjo was persuaded to run for president. His victory convinced many that

Olusegun Obasanjo

Nigeria had turned a vital corner. But over 10,000 Nigerians have died in violent ethnic clashes since 1998, and the country's economic woes have worsened. Obasanjo has been unwilling to tackle the root causes of these problems, and Nigeria's considerable oil wealth still disappears into too many private pockets. He knows that any serious attempt to tackle corruption would probably result in his overthrow, and he has also discovered that ordinary Nigerians will resist attacks on their living standards—fuel-price increases in both 2000 and 2002 brought about **general strikes**.

The Western Media and Africa

On television news programs Africa correspondents stand in front of burned-out buildings, piles of corpses, hospital wards full of buzzing flies and dying children. The images are usually heartrending but rarely placed in context. Africa is portrayed almost exclusively as a disaster zone, but there is little attempt to explain why this should be the case. The other Africa of ordinary people struggling, in often difficult circumstances, to simply get on with their lives, is rarely shown. A small country like Benin, which has been spared natural disasters and widespread human violence and is doing reasonably well, will never be seen or heard from. African news is calamity news.

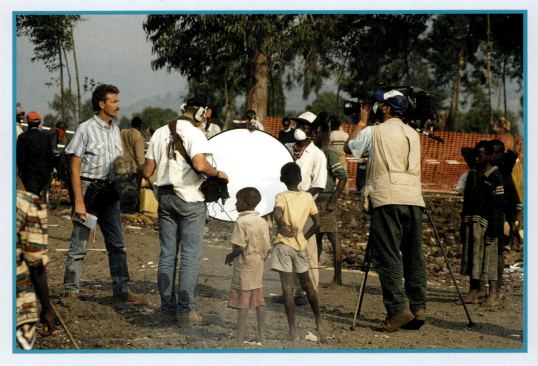

A television crew arrives at a refugee camp in the eastern Congo during the Rwanda crisis of 1994.

The news media are not alone in sticking with **stereotypes**. In Hollywood's earlier days, movies set in Africa were about white men hunting game on the plains, crash-landing aircraft in the desert, or swinging through trees in the rain forest. With a few honorable exceptions, they used Africa as an adventure playground, in which the native animals were considered more interesting than the native humans. In more recent times, mainstream films have concentrated on **colonial** bravery (*Khartoum, Zulu*), wars involving white mercenaries (*The Dogs of War, The Wild Geese*), the struggle against white rule in South Africa (*Cry Freedom, Biko*), and the saving of African animal species from extinction (*Gorillas in the Mist*). Here, too, Western audiences have been left in ignorance of the lives most Africans lead.

Forgotten continent

Perhaps the most telling factor about the media coverage of Africa is how little there actually is. Despite centuries of British involvement in Africa, despite the upsurge in African-American interest in the continent that grew out of the 1960s civil rights movement, news of African events is often hard to come by. The wars in Sudan and Angola dragged on for more than 30 years but rarely received any attention. When peace deals were struck in 2002, media interest was minimal.

Those who run the media might argue that thousands of Europeans, North Americans, and Australians visit **sub-Saharan Africa's** game parks and sites of outstanding natural beauty, yet very few of them choose to venture into the rest of Africa. However, if the fuller picture is not shown, the West will continue to think only of poverty, famine, and disaster when thinking of Africa. Perhaps a more balanced portrayal would encourage more people to see the real Africa.

"Compassion without understanding"

*"Where television is concerned, African news is generally only big news when it involves a lot of dead bodies. The higher the mound, the greater the possibility that the world will, however briefly, send its camera teams and correspondents. Once the story has gone 'stale'—i.e. there are no new bodies and the **refugees** are down to a trickle—the news circus moves on. The powerful images leave us momentarily horrified but largely ignorant, what somebody memorably described as having 'compassion without understanding.'"*
Fergal Keane, from his firsthand account of the Rwandan genocide, Season of Blood: a Rwandan Journey

Turning Point: 2002—Year of Peace?

The year 2002 brought some good news for Africa. Four of the continent's longest-running **civil wars** were brought to an end, at least temporarily. For many observers, long driven to despair by the continent's epidemic of violence, this multiple outbreak of peace seemed like a new dawn.

Giving peace a chance

In Sierra Leone, Foday Sankoh's horrific invasion of the capital, Freetown, in early 1999 was followed by an uneasy **cease-fire** and the dispatch of a **UN** peacekeeping force. In 2000 the war flared up again, and 1,000 British troops were sent to stop Sankoh from retaking Freetown. The rebel leader was captured, and over the next two years the UN forces gradually extended their area of control. By early 2001 most of the rebels had been disarmed. The war was declared over in January 2002, and elections were held the following May. Much of the country was in ruins, but the previous levels of violence and fear had been dramatically reduced.

The Angolan civil war was tilted in the government's favor by UNITA's loss of its Zairean safe haven early in 1998. When UNITA's leader Jonas Savimbi was killed in a gun battle with government troops in February 2002, the heart and drive went out of the rebels. A cease-fire was agreed to in April, and UNITA's army disbanded in August. After 27 years, and at least two million unnecessary deaths, the war seemed finally over.

In July 2002 the two sides in the Sudanese civil war managed, somewhat unexpectedly, to accept a "framework deal" for peace. They would share power for six years. At the end of that period, the inhabitants of the three southern provinces would be allowed to vote for or against a separate state of their own.

In the same month, a deal was struck to end Africa's "Great War." In 2001 Laurent Kabila had been assassinated by one of his bodyguards and succeeded by his son Joseph. Though lacking in experience, Joseph Kabila had soon shown himself to be more interested in peace than his father. In July 2002 he and the Rwandans came to an agreement. In return for Kabila's promise to disarm and deport the Hutu **genocidaires** from the Congo, Rwanda would withdraw its army from Congolese territory within 90 days.

After months of chaos, everyday activities, like shopping in fish markets, have resumed for many in Sierra Leone.

Hopes and fears

Whether, or how long, these peace deals will last is far from clear. The success of the UN intervention in Sierra Leone surprised many observers. Much depends on how successful the newly elected government proves in its attempts to reconstruct the country, both economically and psychologically.

The Sudanese peace deal was the least expected of the four, and it was already fraying badly at the edges by the fall of 2002. The fact that large reserves of oil have recently been discovered in the south makes it unlikely that the deal will stick. It is hard to imagine the north allowing the south to walk away with most of Sudan's potential wealth.

Many observers were equally pessimistic about the deal to end the "Great War," but the Rwandans kept their promise to withdraw their forces from eastern Congo within 90 days. Now, much depends on whether Joseph Kabila's Congolese government can deliver on its side of the bargain.

The Johannesburg World Summit

In August and September 2002, a World Summit on Sustainable Development was held in Johannesburg, South Africa. Its main aims were the reduction of poverty throughout the less **developed** world—of which Africa formed such a large part—and increased protection for the environment. Important agreements were reached to reduce by half the number of people with inadequate sanitation, reduce the use of harmful chemicals, maintain the number of fish in the seas, and halt the extinction of plant and animal species. There was less agreement on how these and other targets were to be achieved. There was also no way of forcing individual countries or corporations to take the steps that seemed necessary. A hundred world leaders addressed the summit, giving some hope for Africa's future. People are eager to try to find solutions to its many problems. Although the outcome at the summit in Johannesburg did not produce any single momentous breakthrough, the results were more comprehensive than any previous outcome.

Children from South Africa, Ecuador, Canada, and China, after addressing the Johannesburg World Summit in September 2002.

Zimbabwe

Some or all of these peace deals may, of course, fall through. In the meantime, other conflicts continue. Liberia often seems on the verge of slipping back into chaos, and Somalia remains at the mercy of its warring **clans**. In the south, the stability and prospects of Zimbabwe and, to some extent, Namibia have been undermined by the incompetence and corruption of their respective governments.

Robert Mugabe has ruled Zimbabwe since 1980, when his ZANU-PF party won the elections that marked the end of the white minority government. Mugabe initially proclaimed his commitment to a democratic, multiracial Zimbabwe, and the white farmers who provided the country with most of its export earnings were encouraged to stay. However, over the next decade, Mugabe created a one-party state and awarded himself increasingly **dictatorial** powers. White-owned farms that fell vacant for one reason or another were generally given to his political allies, rather than divided up between black Zimbabweans in desperate need of land. Mugabe's resemblance to Mobutu grew more pronounced, and Zimbabwe gained a reputation as the latest African kleptocracy.

Zimbabwe's President Robert Mugabe greets supporters during an election rally in June 2000.

The 1990s were hard on African economies. In Zimbabwe corruption and inefficient management made matters worse. As political dissatisfaction rose among the poor black majority, Mugabe tried blaming the country's white farmers and their supporters in the outside world. His followers were encouraged to invade and take over the farms, and several of the farmers were murdered. As lawlessness spread, the economy declined further. In 2002 famine seemed a real possibility.

Mugabe ignored the rulings of his own judges and fixed elections in his own favor. By 2002 he had gone a long way toward destroying the country's political and economic inheritances, for no better reason than keeping himself in power. In the meantime, he and his generals were making the most of the war in the Congo, taking a profitable slice of that country's diamond trade in exchange for protecting the Kabila government.

His example spread to Namibia, where Sam Nujoma's SWAPO lalso came to power after a long **guerrilla** war against the white minority government. Here too, the government seemed more interested in blaming white farmers than in taking the necessary legal steps toward a fairer distribution of the available land. A growing lawlessness was allowed to threaten a tourist industry that provided a sizable portion of the country's income. Namibia's intervention in the Congo, like Zimbabwe's, was mostly an expedition in search of loot.

Mozambique

In recent years, a much more positive example of African development has been provided by Zimbabwe's eastern neighbor Mozambique. Like Angola, Mozambique was given independence by the Portuguese in 1975. Its Soviet-supported government fought a long and destructive guerrilla war against South African–supported Renamo rebels, which was only brought to a peaceful conclusion when both the Soviet Union and white South Africa collapsed. Unlike Jonas Savimbi in Angola, the Renamo leader Alfonso Dhlakama accepted his defeat in elections, and the healing process was allowed to begin. Since then, Mozambique has enjoyed one of the fastest-growing economies in Africa. It has diversified its agriculture, growing cotton, sugar, and cashew nuts for export and a variety of other crops for feeding its own population. Small and medium-sized industries have been successfully launched.

Mozambique has great potential. First, it has peace, which makes everything else possible. Second, it has abundant supplies of energy—coal, gas, and hydroelectric power from the huge Cabora Dam left behind by the Portuguese—that saves the country an enormous amount of money. Third, it has a good government in which corruption is not out of control. Because of these three advantages, the government has been able to provide what international financial institutions like the IMF want—a Mozambique attractive to Western business— without further impoverishing its own people. And this in turn

Two Mozambican women work in a cooperatively owned rice field during the 1990s.

has given rise to a fourth advantage: the West has rewarded Mozambique by giving the country above-average **debt relief**.

Mozambique remains very poor. Life expectancy is only 35 years and 70 percent of its population still live below the **poverty line**. The government must now ensure that all its citizens share in the country's new Western-generated prosperity. If it succeeds in this task—which has proved beyond most African governments— then the future will be bright.

Prospects

Africa's problems are enormous. Who is more to blame for this—the Africans themselves, or the Western powers that control the world economy? Clearly, neither are blameless. **Colonialism** deepened divisions within African societies and froze African economies in a subservient position. In the 40 years since independence, **Cold War** attitudes and Western business interests have ensured that nothing fundamental has changed. But Africans, too, must take some responsibility for the continent's plight. The ruling elites of postindependence Africa have all too often proved **corrupt**, incompetent, and brutal.

Sub-Saharan Africa is caught in a vicious cycle. Economic failure and poverty lead to dislocation and violence, which deter Western companies from investing in Africa's future. Without such investment, failures multiply and poverty deepens. During the 1990s there was an enormous surge of growth in the world economy, but Africa missed out on this growth. There were too many wars, too much havoc, too many safer places for the world's leading corporations and financial institutions to place their investments.

What can be done?

In June 2002 President George W. Bush said "The free people of America have a duty to advance the cause of freedom in Africa." Bush's government, however, has made no attempt to rein in the big multinational corporations, whose unwavering pursuit of profits keeps Africa poor. African coffee growers, for example, receive less than 10 percent of the money U.S. supermarkets charge for a jar of instant coffee, barely enough to cover their costs. The profits are in processing, distribution, and sales, all of which are controlled by the corporations. They have no interest in paying the growers more than they have to.

Only Western consumers have the power to force a change in corporate behavior. Over the last decade, increasing numbers have chosen to buy "Fair Trade" products, which provide the growers with much fairer rewards for their work. Western charities provide emergency support in times of acute crisis and help to supply the knowledge and technology that Africans need to help themselves. Many Western individuals, working through organizations like the American Peace Corps, the British VSO (Voluntary Service Overseas), or the French-based Médicins Sans Frontières (Doctors Without Borders), give their time, effort, and skills to help a continent so much poorer than their own. They work alongside many Africans who are also determined to improve conditions.

Workers on a plantation in Ghana. These organic bananas are sold under a Fair Trade label.

Such aid is enormously valuable, but it can never be enough. In 19th-century Britain, where the poorer section of the population suffered while the rich thrived, people eventually realized that the free market, left to itself, was unable to solve the problem, and would in fact make matters worse. The free market had to be put on hold while those unable to help themselves were given a helping hand. In today's world Africa needs much the same helping hand, but the prospects are not good. Those who thrived in 19th-century Britain needed the labor of those who suffered, and eventually needed their votes to remain in power.

Africa has many resources the world needs and wants, but it does not have a world government to which it can appeal for necessary help. There are, however, reasons to hope. In West Africa, Senegal is peaceful, stable, and relatively prosperous. Nigeria, despite having significant troubles, has recently elected a democratic government. Botswana continues to strengthen its democratic system. And although AIDS is a potentially disastrous problem, Uganda has managed to create a program that has reduced the rate of infection in that country.

Appendix
Chronology of events

1480 Portuguese explore West African coast

1900 Virtually all of Africa colonized

1957–1964 Most sub-Saharan countries in Africa gain independence

1961 Eritrea's struggle for independence from Ethiopia begins

1963 Organization of African Unity (OAU) founded

Civil war breaks out in Sudan

1964 Tanganyika and Zanzibar unite to form Tanzania

1965 Mobutu takes over in the Democratic Republic of the Congo

1967–1970 Civil war in Nigeria

1971 Amin seizes power in Uganda

1972 End of the first Sudanese civil war

1973-1974 Huge oil price increases follow Arab-Israeli War of October 1973

1974 Revolution in Ethiopia

1975 Portugal gives independence to Angola and Mozambique. Civil wars begin in both countries.

1977 Somalia invades Ethiopia's Ogaden region

1978 Amin invades Tanzania

1979 Amin overthrown in Uganda after invading Tanzania

Bokassa overthrown in Central African Republic

1980 Doe seizes power in Liberia

1981 Rawlings seizes power for the second time in Ghana

1983 Second civil war begins in Sudan

1984 Famine in Ethiopia

1989 Civil war begins in Liberia

1990 Central authority collapses in Somalia

Cold War ends. Soviets begin withdrawal from Ethiopia and Angola.

1991 Dergue overthrown in Ethiopia

Agreements to end the civil wars in Angola and Mozambique

Civil wars begin in Sierra Leone

1992 MPLA wins elections in Angola

1993 UNITA restarts civil war in Angola

Eritrea achieves independence from Ethiopia

1994 Genocide in Rwanda

1995–1996 Genocidaires find refuge in the Congo (then called Zaire)

1996 Rwanda invades the Congo in alliance with Laurent Kabila

1997 Congolese leader Mobutu replaced by Kabila

Elections in Liberia

1998 Rwanda invades the Congo for the second time

Obasanjo wins presidential election in Nigeria

1998–2000 War between Ethiopia and Eritrea

1998–2002 Growing Muslim-Christian violence in Nigeria

2002 Peace deals to end civil wars in Sierra Leone, Angola, Sudan, and the Congo

Johannesburg World Summit on Sustainable Development

Further reading

Bingham, Jane. *African Art and Culture.* Chicago: Raintree, 2003.

Binns, Tony, and Rob Bowden. *East Africa.* Chicago: Raintree, 1998.

Bowden, Rob. *The Changing Face of Kenya.* Chicago: Raintree, 2003.

Bowden, Rob, and Roy Maconachie. *The Changing Face of Nigeria.* Chicago: Raintree, 2003.

Reef, Catherine. *This Our Dark Country: The American Settlers of Liberia.* New York: Houghton Mifflin, 2002.

Useful websites

www.amnesty.org

www.africaonline.com

Glossary

Arab member of ethnic group that originated in Arabia and now inhabits much of North Africa and the Middle East

cease-fire agreed end to a period of fighting

Christianity one of the world's three major monotheistic (one God) religions (along with Judaism and Islam) founded by Jesus of Nazareth early in the 1st century

civil war war between different groups in one country

clans social groups based on membership of large, extended families

Cold War period of political hostility from 1945–1990 between the United States and its allies and the Soviet Union and its allies

colonial related to or characteristic of a colony

colonial preference rules of trade that forced colonies to buy from and sell to the European countries that administered them

colony country or area that is ruled by another country

communism political theory and practice that puts the interests of society as a whole above the interests of individuals

constitution in politics, the way a country is set up to safeguard its fundamental principles

corrupt involved in corruption

corruption immoral practices like bribery, fraud, and other forms of financial theft

coup violent seizure of power

debt relief either all or part of a debt being forgiven

democracy political system in which governments are regularly elected by the people, or a country in which this system exists

developed for countries, having a relatively high rate of industrialization or standard of living

dictatorial behaving like a dictator, ignoring anyone else's views or interests

dictatorship unrestricted rule by a single person or small group

ethnic relating to different cultural or racial groups

free enterprise economic and political system in which individuals rather than governments make most of the decisions about which goods and services are produced and how they are bought and sold

general strike refusal of workers in all industries to work

genocidaires those responsible for genocide, particularly that in Rwanda

genocide murder or attempted murder of an entire ethnic group

global warming the gradual warming of the earth's atmosphere, mostly caused by rising levels of carbon dioxide

guerrilla unofficial soldier

human rights rights that should belong to any person

idealistic having the hope and belief that things can be dramatically improved

inflation condition of the economy in which prices of goods and services keep rising

infrastructure material, technological, and economic foundations of a society

Islam one of the world's three major monotheistic (one God) religions (along with Christianity and Judaism), founded by the prophet Muhammad in the 7th century

literacy ability to read and write

military dictatorship government by unelected members of the armed forces

Muslim follower of Islam

Organization of African Unity (OAU) association of African states formed in 1963 for mutual cooperation

persecute treat someone with continual cruelty and unfairness

poverty line level of income, varying from country to country, below which a person is considered to be living in poverty

refugee one who flees for safety, usually to another country

safety zone area in which protection is provided for civilians during a conflict, usually by neutral or foreign troops

shanty town large area of roughly built shelters where the poorest people of a town live

Sharia law collection of laws derived from verses in the Muslim holy book, the Koran

socialism a set of ideas that puts more stress on the needs of the community as a whole and less on the short-term wants or needs of the individual

stereotype typical example, often exaggerated or inaccurate

sub-Saharan Africa region in Africa south of the Sahara Desert

superpower powerful country with more economic, political, and military power than most; usually refers to the United States and the former Soviet Union

trade union organization set up by working people to protect and improve their pay and conditions

tribe social grouping of varying size, which may be based on one or more of several factors, such as language, related clans, ethnic identification, or a shared geographical region

United Nations (UN) international body set up in 1945 to promote peace and cooperation between states

world recession general slowdown of global economic activity (as occurred in the years following the 1973 rise in oil prices)

Index